crying gorgeously; 4:37am

J. Marahuyo

WestWords Books

www.westwords.com.au
41 Hunter Street, Parramatta NSW 2150 Australia.

Published by WestWords Limited 2025.

A catalogue record for this book is available from the National Library of Australia

ISBN: 978-1-923044-46-3
Cover design by Sailor Studio

Printed and bound by Ligare Book Printers
Distributed in Australia by Peribo
5 4 3 2 1

This book is dedicated to my sister, Lashu.

Your light is my guide through life.

J.

ridged & perfect

yawning flora

all vinegar

hysteria & brine

from *Dear Emily* by Emily Skaja

Introduction

Luke Carman

In this debut collection, J. Marahuyo – award-winning, neuro-divergent, Filipino-Australian poet – makes an art of doubling and redoubling: transfiguring hybridised *being* into a *becoming*. The image of 'crying gorgeously' in this collection is an ode to transcendental transmutation. In Marahuyo's subliminations of identity, sexuality, ethnicity, and hybridity, an intimate autobiographical portrait emerges that simultaneously distillates a cosmogonic creation mythos; one complex enough to accommodate the ever-nebulous realities within which we must all make sense of our evolving selves and our ever-increasing, ever-impinging intersections with one another.

From the playful concrete fallopian lineation that opens this anthology, to the 'dark sapphire quark soup ooze' of its star-ship-shaped speculative conclusions, *crying gorgeously; 4:37am* attains multitudes in the poet's associations and dissociations; metamorphosing out of one form and slipping effortlessly into another as she progresses from the cellular zygote, imprinted by the epi-genetics of colonial memory, into the dyadic shock of her original social relations – shadowed all the while by a devouring mother who is half-Hera, half-Cronos – a wicked witch sitting at the centre of a psychic wound like some galactic singularity mistaken for a heavenly body.

At times, the operating logic of these poems is akin to a conceptual hadron collider, walloping images and languages together with such striking intensity and experimental energy that bizarre chimeric associates are brought into being – potent visions of a domestic 'black hole tearing apart an agonised star' appear like 'jump scares' that flash around the dining room walls, orbited by the lost souls of poltergeists, which shimmer as a band of 'dark plasma, bent light, meteorite shrapnel' that are 'hula-hooped' around the malevolent maternal figure's gravitational mass, diffuse with the 'strange particles' of atomised meanings which have wedged themselves between your teeth.

For all their flashing intensities and experimentation, the poet gambols in modes of dark fantasy, 'an ochre forest that fogs the breath and clenches a frigid rivulet', where a 'crumbling goddess' cradles a 'a bowl filled with pink battered brain matter… this incandescent gooey syrup' from which the Divine Mother occasional feasts. Vivid vignettes of social life are populated with faerie tale vocabularies, poisoned apple iconography, ill-fated fae-folk chorus lines, Prince Charming drunk on Twilight's laughter, Golden Geese co-habitants, and entire aviaries of anthropomorphic bird life, all giving rare wings to the political and personal dimensions of this self-portraiture in an array of unexpected amalgamations and migrations.

Thrumming through the traumatised and tear-slicked contours of these lines is a profound depth of longing, and the hero of this poetic journey is perhaps a resplendent demonstration of transcendental desire. An aching evocation of unfiltered Eros courses along the forms and features of the latter poems like an orgastic heartbeat, going beyond merely 'perfect princes' who subsist simply 'to lure you; to inhabit (you)r lovely deliriums of a lost self', reaching for that eternal state of 'celestial twinkling'. And onward still, beyond the domains of sex and submission, gravitating toward some grand hybrid visions in verse, where you, dear reader, are right where the poet wants you, subject to her fierce 'ambrosial waves', as she delivers a reckoning: 'watch my humantics, my rhythmic blaze, how I dare danger'. Marahuyo's debut is an arrival for the poetry of our shared time and place; an anthem for readers who feel themselves illumined by her daring.

Luke Carman *is an Australian fiction writer and academic best known for his collection of semi-autobiographical stories,* An Elegant Young Man. *His stories are set in the suburb of Liverpool, Western Sydney. He has been recognized as a post-grunge lit writer, a reference to an Australian literary genre from the 2000s that emerged after the 1990s grunge lit genre.*

I. HELLO, NIGHTMARES.
Once Upon a Time 2
Living within the Accretion Disk 4
She cradles a bowl 9
I am welcoming myself 10
Infinite Blue Candies and Eyeballs 13
whisper thank you to their king-sized bed for not swallowing them; 19
i'm an anxious caterpillar 23
anger as a poison apple 27
Happiness 28
Blessings From the Pious 29
Absolve me 30
A charming squirrel's acorn 31
What even are we? 33

II. BREAK ME, I BOUGHT IT.
Never's Interlude 38
2:00am 41
The Allure of Never 42
Pristin-ity 44
Oceanic Kink 45
He, a frosty suckle driver 46
4:37am; crying gorgeously 48
coral reefs 50
Workplace Boundaries 51
2:22pm. crying. dramatically. 52
sheet lightning 54

Fistfuls of Sand 55
the eye of desire's storm 62
Honey Bee 63
Lustrous mind 64

III. *SINGS LOUDLY WHILE DANCING ALONE*
stop making yourself cry 68
ba-ad ba-ad black sheep 70
meeting Amihan 72
not pamilya enough to be 74
My time as a goldfish 75
Memories of rain 76
You don't look filo 78
ambrosial waves 80
I nearly crushed my dog to death 84
Frankie, the cat. 86
Flame Bowerbird 88
the bird that could not fly 89

IV. DÉJÀ RÊVÉ
We bought a star 95

Notes 98
Acknowledgements 99

I.

HELLO, NIGHTMARES.

Once Upon a Time

I was there, divided,

oocyte and sperm

in the everlasting

teenage dream of a

party, of booze, of

lack of supervision; lack

of pamphlets and diagrams in textbooks

depicting what happens when

you insert the penis

into the

vagina

and

e j a c u l a t e. The holy Bible spurted,

impregnating Filipinos en masse,

from the first 16th century Spanish

M I S S I O N A R Y is how I unwillingly

picture my conception unlike

the unwanted, wriggling image from

when I was seven: you see, we were meant to go

to the movies yet
I sat waiting in front of
the TV for one and a half
hours before finally out of
patience walked up to their open

unlit room
and my eyes adjusted to their
blanket bound bodies
shifting,   shift i n g,

s h i f ting,

s h i   f t i n g

so   I sat back down,
stared blankly at
the screen and learnt
to wait,

their needs were always the priority

Living within the Accretion Disk

Mother was so bright
I mistook her for the sun
with her radiant smile that reached
the eyes of all
in her vicinity. Some would
chase, some would stare
and those bewitched would waft
her praises through the air.

Though, no one could ever see
the band of dark
plasma, bent light, meteorite
shrapnel which hula-hooped her body. Being
swept in her orbit meant
hearing a poltergeist or two.
(It might explain why those who stayed
were very few). At
times I found strange
particles in my teeth, morsels
of mean

or felt lost

stuck
in
s
l
o
-
m
o

complete unreality.

And, I
never felt warm,
only a squeeze in my throat
that sluggishly
s
t
r
e
a
k
e
d

my
cheeks
when anyone spoke to me.
I always hoped no
one would question or
notice.

With every question came
Something.
Something was wrong.
Something nagged.
Something spouted gibberish,
and danced downside, inside, through
Mother's words screaming,
'WICKED!'
Something kneed me in my shins.
Something flipped,
lipping bleeps
that came from sheep,
and Something called Mother
a bitch.
Something knew
something I didn't know.

The closer I stared into every refracted memory
I saw light
did not emanate from her.
Instead, it dangled,
ensnared in her circling debris
forgotten by their owners, her
ex-friends, ex-coworkers, ex-s.
With my half locked eyes focused on the floor,
I like to believe confusing her for radiance
instead of a singularity engulfing
those enamored was an easy mistake to make.

When I rounded the wall
that blocked the stairs from the living -
and dining room allowing for jump scares, I saw

a black hole tearing apart
an agonised star
my sister crying
as mother towered over her
threatening through gritted teeth
that she'll give her

something

to

c

r

y

about.

Mother's fingers twisted
into her seven year old skin
left curved flickers of red
next to yellow-haloed, purple-
black
voids.

Mother promptly spun her head
towards me, her face
a flash of crooked rage.

Averting my eyes
and pretending to smile
I greeted her as if I had seen
nothing at all.
But, she knew
I knew.

She cradles a bowl

The place I am dragged to
when I close my eyes is an ochre forest
that fogs the breath
and clenches a frigid rivulet.

Past the clusters of dried, rolled leaves
and frosted grass,
lifeless trees genuflect
to a stone statue, Virgin Mary-esque.

The crumbling goddess's glazed stare
fixates on

emptiness.

She cradles a bowl
filled with pink battered brain matter, euphoria.
This incandescent gooey syrup
the only thing unfrozen.

Every so often she dips her hand in
and brings it to her lips.

I am welcoming myself

I know who I am only in relation
to you, Mother.
Your perpetual barbs hold up a mirror:
a lazy, inconsiderate ingrate
watches magical maternal wrists
flick material, bought affections,
their fragile meanings up, over the banister,
rolling down the carpet river
to meet the white tiles of the kitchen
where sharp tools gather
for another chance to carve
love on my left cheek.
The word rings and rings, out-ringing
all else, as if in worship.

I am kneaded, dyed,
my jumble of limbs coerced to fit,
cookie cutter clean.
You wove the word *perfect* within
me while I was an embryo,
each follicle a mythical signal
to those gathering.

\- Yet, I don't seem to have the craft
for spinning spit or pitting pining people,
at least, not the way you do, Mother.

I study your spells, copy the way
you cantillate.
I drink each vial you say I'll like
the bursts of sadness, humiliation
and dependence on your forest green
apples with their colours so pretty,
pulp so pleasing.

You leave me lacking after
each divine retribution.

I need to be your Mini-Me
which means thinking meagrely,
echoing petty things right up until
I grow too big for the tiny space
in the house you so adore.
So comes the swat, swat, swat.
Mother, you swat me down.
When you turn away
I fly through the vastness,

flurry with nightmares, sunshine, heathens.
None of which are as terrifying
as staying a Mini-You.

I am welcoming myself, the Villain.
A crowning deal for popping each socket
replacing all these fingers and toes
bleaching every thread on my scalp.
Though, I am still in the middle of yanking
out my eyes,
re-frying my brain.
I have almost completed the restitch
to be my own glorious and refined other:

Villain.
How do you like it,
my ginormous antagonistic
capital V?

Infinite Blue Candies and Eyeballs

Panoptes

Mother with her gilded champagne hair,
seemingly infinite blue eyeballs, needed no cameras,
not when she had a real time feed from her
many plucked out eyes discreetly hidden in immaculate
room top corners, in any book that had o's
and in all door knob key holes.
But, best of all, was in the skull
of the doll that roamed the house
recording every movement, every word spoken
whenever Mother was not home.

Doll:

The doll walked into our lives,
built a house, drove us to school.
My sister, Buwan, and I would chat to it
wanting to be welcoming, warm. One afternoon
Mother commented we were great entertainment,
beckoned the doll over, plugged its eyes into the projector
showed us a clip of that morning's events.
We stopped being friendly.
We spent the first 40 minutes of the following x years
staring out the car window
watching traffic snake around houses, the sun stalk
us before we got out
and grumbled gratitude.

Mother loved to boast of the doll's endless supply
of pure gold eggs,
each more delicious than the last, she said.
We were never allowed a taste.

Family:

In my 13th year a new baby came,
tucked in a manger, almost
lost in the mail. He was
the most beautiful baby brother.
The doll's makers: a couple of golden geese
came to live with us, one exclaimed they would be called
'lolly' to pay homage to our heritage and the other
did not bother feigning interest.
Buwan and I were excited to meet new family
so we chattered, quizzed,
but Mother pulled us aside and said,

"Stop bothering them. They don't want to talk
to either of you.
They're here for their only grandson. "

Buwan continued with her questions.
Me? I slunk up to my room,
laid in bed and sent my thoughts
to the fairy realm with my hand reaching for
the ceiling, turning it periodically, wondering
if someone, somewhere would ever kiss my palm.

Buwan:

Buwan liked to antagonise, just a little,
leaving notes on her door like,
'Not today, I'm tired',
knowing Mother would react
with a shout that caused the house to tremble
before charging in anyway,
to make sure Buwan met her
quota of tears for the day.

When Buwan cried it was through
a cold glare
and a toss of black hair
Mother never left until Buwan waned,
shat out a smile.

Mother's Mirror:

Every so often Mother would brush my hair.
Today was a little different as she stared at my
changing body,

"Now that your breasts and hips are coming through
I think it's best if I start collecting your tears too.
A new job. A new title. Think of it
as a promotion
my pretty little flower,
my perfect echo."

Yes was the only acceptable answer.
She rewarded me with a sparkling blue
candy, popping it into my mouth. I turned
to the mirror, saw my pink insides
stain silvery blue
which always perked her up.
Mother took my chin and turned my head
so I was facing her again
her infinite blue eyeballs reflected brilliantly
against my metallic mouth.

(Mother doesn't know
Buwan has been stealing
small golden eggs from the doll.)

"Who is the most wise?"
Mother is.

"Who is always right?"
Mother is.

"Who knows everything?"
Mother does.

whisper *thank you* to their king-sized bed for not swallowing them;

after ali whitelock

the light caught trees dripping
with aureate fish dangling
by their caudal fins,
cheerily bidding adieu in billows. they
usher the waking of stars
yawning maidens
stretch languidly;
their smiles twinkle as dreams
and nightmares glimmer
behind windows, flickering bulbs,
eyelids
of children who've
tucked themselves in.

the lucky ones may dream of bonfires
feeding into blazing friendships;
of booming elephants who play
rhinestone trombones for troupes of sewer rats
the rats dance jazz as they conga
toward clusters of asteroids;
where blessings of narwhals spiral chariots
over cosmic islands home to dark
matter beluga whales.

*

one child will wake, perhaps
not wanting to.
whisper *thank you*
to their king-sized bed
for not swallowing them;
the child recalls their mother's and father's
conversation about the guest
they helped nurse back to health.
today is the day they will
set it free.

*

the child creeps
to the laundry room
where a temporary nest,
a basket full of blankets,
holds a small bird.

the child pleads

with it to stay

just o n e l a s t d a y;

the child reaches in, pulls

a tail feather,

flusters when the bird

jolts and yips;

tries to soothe it with

sorrysorry i'm so sorry.

the child shrinks

out of the room,

reasons their absence

will calm the bird.

*

before leaves transform
into aureate fish
the mother whose eyes
see infinite monsters,
mentions the bird;
the bird could not reach
the height of blue.

she says,
it became cat food.

the mother's eyes land.

the mother places questions
made of dark matter on the child;

the child crawls to bed,
shivering.

i'm an anxious caterpillar

a journal   with sturdy, wide arms
enveloped and   soaked me in
allowing me   to rest,
hidden   from the world.

i would spend   days
laying   on its blue lines
letting myself   untangle
into graceful curves   of an 's'
the folded butterfly   of an 'f'
the bold loops   of 'y's

in my naivety i   believed
no one   would be interested
in the   ramblings of a preteen
so i did not   hide my journal
well   enough

a witch   was about
and secrets were   her favourite
dish   to serve

she found my journal
under my pillow
she lifted it and
shook out bits
of my voice
to feed to her
pet parrots

finding my words
blotting out the newspaper
as shit at the bottom of cages,
on the floor of the living room,
on the grass in the backyard
of another house at a party

caused me to wilt:
my thoughts are leaking;

tip of my tongue
compulsively restrained
between teeth as unconsciously as
synapses firing.

always checking,
checking, checking,
a little press, a little pain to know,
yes, yes my tongue is still there,
still, still between.

in the middle
of my own silent battle
a parrot with
downward, mocking crescent eyes
came pecking for
answers, *Who is this -*
this one you say you love?

his name which i had
never spoken,
not even to him was flapping
from this parrot’s beak.

unable to let thoughts bathe,
my voice was held for a decade
in the witch's grip.

my over-thoughts
escape through shaking legs,
crossing-un crossing toes;
cold clammy palms; dead
skin from restless fingers
flaked from scrapes
by anxious thumbs.

anger as a poison apple

w
o
r
d
always s waggering
dousing each ember, flicker, sparkle of poise
placing shards of hot rock fragments from volcanoes
which pierce and cause decay like the big and burly who
rush forth to show who's boss, breaking the surface tension
keeping me wrapped snug, keeping my ribs predictable. the spill-
age transforms each extremity into spectres flinging last
night's pizza boxes, dead fish, picture frames; cream en-
crusted dishes, bug spray, chicken bones. the unrelenting
seismic pressure either snags a pair of scissors
piercing the heart of the mattress or makes do with
a trio of fingernails to make welts but should
that not suffice a ghastly inclination to
bang the back of my head on
the wall appeases.

Happiness

A woman in her crumpled cotton dress
has light steps, bare feet

powdered with dirt and mud and maybe
a little dark chocolate cake.

If you glimpse her you'll see iridescent hair,
lavender blushes and glimmers.

She loves to frolic, pull off toupees. She darts
from linen cupboards and echoes shadows,

fusing with punched-then-plastered walls
just when I think I've caught her,

leaving no smudge, no trail or rain scent.
I become ragdoll heavy.

Eyelids sinking. Drenched.

When I ply them open I see her waiting,
smiling, and eager to start the next game.

Blessings From the Pious

I walk, heat beat, on the footpath off the side of Great Western Highway pretending my umbrella is another pair of shoulders shielding me from the world's red swastika vandalised walls. I try to hide my spasmodic sobs, snotted face. *I'm okay. I'm okay. I'm not there anymore.* I hear a woman's voice hail with worry. My embedded deference outweighs my need for space so I meet her well intentions. I allow her to comfort me with her loving god.

I'm too touched to say I don't share her faith. So I nod, thank her instead. She gives me her number, vows she'll introduce me to Filipinos, mistaking my quiet for lonely. Later, she sends a message: God loves all his children,

God bless

is also what my psychologist keeps ending sessions with even after I tell her it makes me uncomfortable.

Absolve me

‘Is it because your mum
    doesn’t   love   you?’,

words, not mine.

Something I never acknowledged,
birthed,
                    blood-soaked,
                                        screaming.

She goes on explaining
‘Some people are just
incapable.’ I nod

and nod and
the certainty she bears
bores dead-eyed
deep   into
my   consciousness.

A charming squirrel's acorn

after the Ice Age movies

We could blame the fissure of Pangaea
on an animated squirrel's acorn, defying
logic the way an ear-inserted funnel can
annex reality only so long as a constant
stream of debris gushes to overpower
what is already known.

What is known
becomes alien like a curled up towel-
cloaked child at the foot of a bed stealing
time and warmth for the day to come while
trying not to disturb her sleeping Lola.
The child mistakenly dozes off,
her wet hair growing
into a dark halo on the sheet unlike

the blob of laway bestowed
on top of a strawberry kiss hanging
on her Lola's sagging cheek
turning Lola into an angry
animated squirrel —
the child, now grown,
outpacing her halfhearted wallop.

The grown woman sees Lola
see-saw from old lies to new
and exhale them as if they were truth.

As if watching the squirrel plunge his acorn
into the centre of the Earth, dividing its continents,
the woman is watching her Lola do the same to her,
like she is a creature deserving the stake.

The grown woman

cr/ acks { bre}aks fis-sures

sunders between an onslaught of emotions:

longing for her childhood protector

acorn-fuelled anger

acceptance toward the possibility

of never

reuniting

with her Lola again.

What even are we?

I remember calling you Donkey Kong
because it matched your initials.
And, you called me 'Ate' *(ah-teh)* -
big sister in tagalog
because our culture is big on respect,
big on our titles for those older,
but I'm not sure what else.

As your older cousin
I did a poor job, didn't I?
When I showed that hand, our family magic.
(I didn't know it was a secret, but
I've learnt intentions really don't matter).
That flashy crystal my mum used to love
to parade around on school day drives and shopping trips,
'Your uncle is addicted to methamphetamines,
Tsk, always asking your grandma for money.'

I laughed the way she did when I casually
mentioned your dad's time on ice
not knowing how inappropriate until
I saw you blank
then blink
and say, 'Oh.

… I didn't know.'
You recounted how he would disappear for months;
no one ever told you, or your brother, anything.

Sometimes he'd show up only to leave.
You thanked me, you finally knew why.

We said we'd meet again
and we waved each other off.
I stared at the sky blurred with periwinkle blue
and delicate white
as I replayed the day on my way home.
I had finally seen you for the first time in years.

My dad messaged me
saying to leave your family alone
as if I had shoved you all in a box
and shaken the whole goddamn thing.

Your dad took over your phone
telling me he would get me.
How he knew someone who worked at the
Roads and Maritime Service;
he'd get my address.
How I'll never see you again.
How my father was no angel;

he had done it too.
But, here's the difference:
I knew.
Not that he had dabbled in meth,
he was always shrouded in smoke,
maybe I just didn’t have any expectations.
So, I didn't care. At least,
I tried not to.

Perhaps our fathers,
being immigrants, were easy enough prey
to the helplessly sweet caress
of a seemingly endless haze,
a glass full
of always happy
or perhaps it was a self-aware hesitation
toward the direction they were running.

I don’t know when it started
but I hate being Filipino.
Everyone is always loud
but not about things that actually matter.
Everyone always cares
but only so they can talk about you later.
Everyone always wants to sing.

Have you noticed at every Filipino party
there is always a karaoke machine?

I spoke to my therapist of my sudden urges to sing,
And he said it was a release: a way to gather oxygen,
and blow out the stale emotions.
Who knows if it's true -
god? He doesn't bother me anymore.

Maybe, all of us are a muscle, drumming
and navigating this erroneously mapped,
copper landscape with song.

Maybe, it's a shared subconscious trying to clear
and make way for something better than the past.

Or maybe we're all just so traumatised,
don't recognise it
and just keep belting tune after tune.
Everything hidden under layers of
of loudness and oily, fatty, delicious, fried food.

You and I, we should be careful,
heart attacks pulse through our family.
It's the leading cause of death in The Phils;
it transverses oceans
and is gasping to find
another rhythm.

II.

BREAK ME, I BOUGHT IT.

Never's Interlude

In this sphere where Twilight sings
Prince Charming and I were suspended, drunk
on each other's laugh
we watched the faeries twirl, then I
stumbled for his amusement.

Twilight asked The Prince if he could ever love me.
Maybe

As Twilight's aria of magenta,
indigo and marigold grew
everlasting, a woman separate from me
swayed wanton and brazen in my body.
She smirked as a forest
of sleep engulfed me.

The faeries watching from Twilight's back
cheered and emboldened the wanton woman.
Hmph, she thought, *Of course they find delight*
in someone as mesmerising as me.

The faeries silhouettes mirrored her dance
and rage uncoiled across her face
as she wanted his eyes; their eyes;
all eyes
to follow only **her**.

Pouting, she stripped, reached for the Prince
who professed his fear in his lust for her.
All she knew was to please.
She was ever, ever eager.

The blooming heart
I had carefully, sweetly, tended
was her first victim. She wiped the blood
on Twilight's skirt causing the sky
to roil in merlot.
Delirious from the kill
she begged him
to fuck her.

The Prince replied,
Holy shit, you're such a good girl.

Then, he took a moment to consider her request.
Maybe, he said, as he let her drink
his thorn apple voice,
stones sank straight to her navel.

The woman separate from me took
over Twilight's song
which crashed like collapsing cymbals.
The umbels shivered in her arrogance.
The faeries made fun.
She chased the teasing faeries,
strangled the ones caught.

Twilight's gaze dripped
soaking the sky in a starless stain.

The woman, terrified by the sudden
loss of light,
called for Prince Charming who gave no answer.
He had slipped away
once her chaos had satisfied
his want of entertainment.

Panicked, she tripped on the faeries' dead bodies
wailing my name.

2:00am

Me:

bet you didn't know
you kept me up all night
not leaving until I felt
myself clench around my vision
of your two constricted fingers

*

You:

you're kicking the blanket off
after an urge a half-moon peek
at me vulnerable
hands tied supple defiant
on the verge of
melting

The Allure of Never

The perfect prince

is sustained
in - between -
in places effortlessly
out of   reach

hidden behind
airy eyes;
acknowledged only
in the ███
where the   absence
of him is

most

S
E
N
S
U
A
L

The perfect prince

resides where he is almost ~~real.~~
within the one who is both
narrator and soubrette.

He is

marble, minutely carved,
waltzing through

h w
ollo

ballrooms enveloped in
strawberry milk clouds.

The perfect prince

~~lives~~
to lure you;
to inhabit (you)r
lovely deliriums of
a lost

s

e

l

f

Pristin-ity

My   pristine canvas

   let me   ignore you

into   perfection.

You   my pristine perfection

   ignore me.

My ignorant   canvas

   let me bleed into you,

   let me   imperfect

         your pristin-ity -

       pristine you into me,

perfection.

Oceanic Kink
after Paris Rosemont

As a woman
I want you to take me.
Recognise my power, make me feel
Inferior but only
With my permission.

You should
Murmur real
Affection into my bones
As kindly as you can to
Capsize the harshness
Of the act

Like oceanic curves and tidal
Destruction -
Do not do it

If you cannot be responsible

For my lustrous mind.

He, a frosty suckle driver

I step into a winter evening, watch
garra rufa fish swim through
smoke from my 'O' shaped mouth. audible
breath. They bunch to suckle heat, take turns
to slap my round cheeks with frosty fins -
some even do it to my nose

I step into the Uber,
say hi to the driver,
look over to see small
brush strokes of a sleeve
on the fogged window.
I stare out,
pretend I'm a stranger, stepping into the
house overspilling mood and music
make my way to the back
to hug a friend
take a hit from the passing joint

e v e n i n g f r i e n d overspilling to a s l o - m o

He, a frosty suckle driver

fogged back stare
hitting my 'O' sentences

I step
Hi eyes

Shape. sleeve slap.

take pretend step
to Stranger

I roll into a hug

step on leg sleeve

audible slap of Judgment,
stroked with chill

I step
turn my fogged brain into some sentences

I'm a mood,   slap,   step,
make face 'O'

shaping winter through my s l o - m o hugs

suckling on a man made of smoke

I swim, fish-step

I   a fish   swimming to alone

step, watch: heat leaving   through nose

I   s t a r e   into

forgetting

I. am. the. evening. watching.

I'm the car
and the mood,

light leaving

4:37am; crying gorgeously

My chest echoes my sweet
-est 2022 November scene

on repeat;
my ribs fill, de-
flate, re-
fill with two words:
You're gorgeous
uttered by a man
on a warehouse lined road,
inside a streetlamp's blade,
on the backseat
of his car;

those two words
hassled each thought.
I dug my nails into them as

my concept of light flitted; as
I savoured my
airy state.

the scene is
so breathtaking-
ly dismal;
my first un-fished
compliment
g o r g e o u s
in my orbit.
I had emerged
from a 10 year
relationship
a month prior

it makes me -
?   !   :):   @#\%asdfghj

I release the ultramarine
butterfly-memory;

then I
grab it
mid.   -   flight
yank off
its wings;

drop its stiff, curled body
into a vantablack tube

coral reefs

you speak   with the vibrancy   of coral reefs

abundant   with mauves

darting marigold fish

colonies of   bone-brown plums   reaching upward

all resonating   with fluorescence

I   with the heat   of the sun

shy behind

sharp white   clouds

knowing   my prolonged radiance

would   bleed you   blanch.

Workplace Boundaries

I have been practising how to breathe (*IN*-one-two-three) / so I can re-focus on
my screen (*OUT*-four-five-six) / as I reprimand my irises / lungs / frontal lobe
/ all seized by your presence -

its potential spurs my fantasies / during my solitary winter afternoons /
handcuffing me to / my vibrator / but - I still won't dare / unravel your name /
even as I / add to the condensation running / down the windows

maybe I could write / all my thoughts / fold them small / enough to fit into /
your ear - yet I really / really hope / you don't notice

my desire / to see a little violence / in those gentle eyes of yours / my
predisposition to feel / a continuous pouring of you / onto the softness of my
skin / down my throat / into the cusp / of elevation -

have you stroke the excess / with your thumb / up my chin / into my mouth / as
you command /
Drink
it
up

2:22pm; crying. dramatically.

i am mortal once more. hydrangea-bruises
cloud; my skin like
viole(n)t streaks of sunset.
made alkaline·pretty
by the plumes of
a faraway
volcano.

Our eruption was
here, not
ready, ex-

Act I: My wish - a molten
summer, my abandon
above the mesosphere.

like a white shirt heavied
by the ocean's foam
my soul is translucid
on my breasts.

a mirage: a fountain
of kisses
marooned my ·c·he.eks·
left my ○h:an.ds··
coated in sand

·(Now, I look up. ·
.. a .year later
my eyes do not dew
the way my audacity ·does) ○
○ ○ ⁚ ⁛ ⁛ . .⁚ · ○ ··○ ⁚ . · ·
... .··. ·.○ . . ⁚ . . · . · · .
·○. Q: *Why are you crying* ○ · · . . . · ·
· *into your pillow, again?* ⁚ . . · ·
· · · .. ⁚ . · . . ·
○ . · ·· . · i want to · ○ ⁚ ⁚ ·.. ○·.
. smoke a joint, ○ · ⁚ · . ○
. hidden inside ○. . · . ·⁚ ·
· . a bobby pin container · · · · · .. ⁚
○⁚ . · .. ○. · ... . · ⁚ ·⁚ . ·
: i want to unlatch its hot pink lid. · · · ·
·. ○. · . · ○i want to . ⁚ ..
· . . sleep and not · · · ○ ⁚ ⁚
⁚ . . ⁚ .· . dream . ⁚ ○. ..
○· ·○⁚ .··.○ . .. ⁚ ... ·.○ · ○ ⁚ ⁚·.. ○·.○ .
. ·· . ·· · . ○ ○ ⁚ ⁚
. ○. · . ·⁚ ⁚ · . . ○ ○ ⁚ ⁚ .· .· .· ..⁚ · ○ ··○ ⁚ . ··
. ... ⁚ . .
· · ⁚ · · .. .○...· ○
⁚
.
.. · . · .

sheet lightning

you casually lean
shoulder resting on the wall

I notice the way
your shirt clings

your voltaic atmosphere
aching to shock

my impressionable skin
my fraught nipples

my stirring hands
competing in tug-of-war

with my self-control

my consuming carnality   flashing
to dispel space

and char
the air

Fistfuls of Sand

~~ ✧ ~~ ✧ ~~ ✧ ~~ ✧ ~~ ✧ ~~ ✧ ~~ ✧ ~~ ✧ ~~

We   drove away
the midnight

fishers with the   innocence
of our   existence

clingingtooneanother   like   we

hadn't just   met

speaking of   goals   your
six year plan to   settle down

me   not knowing
if I ever would

like we weren't there
just to fuck

'You were so
loud I could hear
your moans echoing'

Half a joint

later he's talking

when he should

be **touching**

I slide his hand

from around my

waist past my

v u l v a

so his fingers

are on my

c l i t

He and I are
face to face.

His fingers are
curious. He finds
what he’s after

and I cum
for the first time that night.

He doesn’t leave me
stranded as his fingers
lure and liberate

my opulence.

I don’t know
anything. I am

o r g a s m i c A celestial

twinkling. I am salt
and sand

I am the lick
of the ocean reaching
for dry land.

I was the heat
missing from his
midnight dreams.

~~ ✧ ~~ ✧ ~~ ✧ ~~ ✧ ~~ ✧ ~~ ✧ ~~ ✧ ~~ ✧ ~~

I release
fistfuls of sand

you use my
arms as leverage
to pull me to
Reverse Cowgirl

I let you watch
my ass bounce
I let you watch
my ass jiggle

as I unmask and become
Tala.

moan. moaN. moAN. mOAN. MOAN. *M O A N*

~~ ✧ ~~ ✧ ~~ ✧ ~~ ✧ ~~ ✧ ~~ ✧ ~~ ✧ ~~ ✧ ~~

Shooting stars.
How do you feel?
I tried to make a wish
All I could think was
The sky is a navy knit
I may have made a wish
I don't remember.

SECTION IN PROGRESS

Moment of clarity:
Oh. My. God. You're fucking
me right by the ocean.

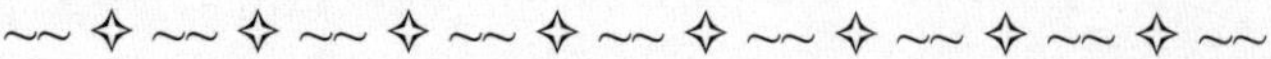

mmm-I'm-cumming-its-so-good-mmmm-please.
Please.

Please.

OHMYGODFUCK!

*Yes-YES-Mmmm-mmm-Mmmmmmm-please-ahh-Mmm-I'm-Ah-mmmm-Ohfuck-Ohfuck-Ah-ah-Ahhhh-*AHHHHHH-I'm-cumming-again-AH-AHHHH-AHHhh-mmmmm-YES-ahhh-ohmyfuckinggod-*ahhhhhhh-mmmm-nnnnnnn-mmmnnnnnn-ohhhh-oh-oh-oh-nnnnnn-*mm-nnnnnnnngggg-pleasepleaseplease-ah-PLEASE-*mmmmm-MMM-ah-Ah-AHHHH-mnnnmmmmmm-FUCKYES-AH-HAH~-mmmnng...*

One after the
other bubbles of solace
rise. Each prod and shift
of dick pricks their
e f f e r v e s c e n c e.
They travel from my
f a l l o p i a n t u b e s,
soar over my tongue and
s c a t t e r

into
the
night.

~~ ✧ ~~ ✧ ~~ ✧ ~~ ✧ ~~ ✧ ~~ ✧ ~~ ✧ ~~ ✧ ~~

He lifts someone who bears my likeness.
He places his arms under her pits like
she were a scarecrow made of only straw.
He pulls her back so she's sitting again.
He offers her water. She asks him to put
the bottle to her mouth.
He lifts the bottle.
She drinks.

My seaweed peppered lips
taste like hibiscus and honey

~~ ✧ ~~ ✧ ~~ ✧ ~~ ✧ ~~ ✧ ~~ ✧ ~~ ✧ ~~ ✧ ~~

the eye of desire's storm

cup my nape like you're ready to drink
the morning chill from my tongue's
embrace me

like a precious memory
of a present that could have been.

desperate to feel, you grab what you can:
the salience of my hips,
my juice-able rear.

you leave your scent in my hair, specks
under my nails, teeth marks that stay tender

Honey Bee

I like the dizzying high,
the floral invitations
my belly, home to bees
my eyes, honey-filmed

I crumble in my foraging nature,
from my honeycombed mind,
to my body royal with lust,
from the sting of my own touch

to

my
sour
actuality

Lustrous mind

for Finn O'Branagain

In bed:
I asked him   to call me   a slut.
I asked him   to treat me
like a whore.

Out of bed:

he kept on
spitting in my
mouth.

Now I see
others beaming with true
endearment and I can't
help but wonder

Is this the right
kind of love
for me?

I am a lighthouse peeking
into the fog -
ged up window of a car.
Their touch is.   Animalistic.
No inspiration
reverberates in the discs
of her serpentine spine.

Finn asks,
Do you want a hug?

Their warmth punctures
my surface tension
mid-hug
No one else would ever
love me.
I'm a disintegrating
coastline.

Finn asks,
What qualities
are you drawn to?

Often when we're infatuated
we are searching for
ourselves

Finn asks,
What qualities do you admire —
Can you apply them to yourself?

Kindness in my voice
Warmth in my eyes
Fluency in my language
Care for those around me

Finn says,
The love you're yearning, give it to
yourself.

III.

SINGS LOUDLY WHILE DANCING ALONE

stop making yourself cry

,

A*

sad N ess

= ille G 'al =

∞offensE, punish-

able/you aRe WRONG

,'i howdareyoubeyou!

emotions(hidden) i'

uncontrollable

'

N

r A w

di/s T ress

an ab U ndant

& vital R elease

i urgently'A ctivated:

daily.bio L ogically

' reasoned,simple '

' i' relief

'

R'

' fr E ed,

' actu A l'feels

, libera L ly,real'ly

salty∘ streaked '

, palpable truth',

clear& real'

· o'N ⦚ ,

child's/ Emotions

raise ↑max Guilt + shame

4outcome=subLiminal message

=u do not mattEr¡!¡=less than,

' (u)*insignifiCance seen in /

thru adul'T'hood ⦚ ¡

, H ,

' n Eed

,◦ valuA ble¡⦚

hormoneL eveling

sign of sT rength,¡¡

↑empatHy↑reco-

verY ♥ ,

ba-ad ba-ad black sheep

I am sad,
very, very sad, *but*
I am
the sharpest little lamb.

I am bad news.
The flock warns: do not go
too close.

So, if you were to grow too
close
inquisitive
careless,
my ink would seep
into your nail beds.

You would speak
like me:
backboneblack
on stark white pages.

I am bold
against the regurgitated green
apple skins
surrounding my feet,
poison, I purged.
Unashamed, I will blow
vomit alloyed kisses
in your direction.

Then, the family hand
gripping the back of my neck
I will amputate and stab
with bitter glee.
And, you,
you'd be witness
to its helpless writhing.

You'll ask me why,
I'll meet your eyes,
offer you a smile,

so the moon,
see,
so the moon
can blossom

meeting Amihan

for ate p

You who is free
chose my windowsill

to describe your honeysuckle dreams

feet on the ground head above mine

You spoke in royal blue

beak closed your yellow eyes recognising me

despite the madness

of my form

your diaphanous thoughts

gliding from culm- to- culm

fledgling infernos

against a backdrop of bamboos

reassuring me

mayroong lakas at kagandahan

in teetering steps

in the netted wings of a damselfly in the space between each mortal body

(that space)

between us all

is the same as the space between each galaxy

//

look You said *look at how blades of grass run*
holding hands

knowing they'll be okay wherever the journey halts

if one stills with unease the rest will stop
they'll stay and play
until each one is ready for another pace

take time to tousle them with your toes so they may

tickle your soles
with their own oscillating souls

not pamilya enough to be

Donkey Kong, kumusta ka?
I miss you whenever I happen to
think of you. How can I not?
Our childhoods were spun together:
                    ako;   looking after you
                    ikaw;   looking after your baby brother,
                    changing his nappies
                    in Lola's red brick apartment.
                    No one else in sight.

Then, I think *what if*
I only think of you
                    because you're the safest to think about?
What if   you're just a distraction
                    to my kettle hissing;   pot of emotions;
                    a distraction from our pamilya.

                    Donkey Kong,   you're
                    one click   away.
Between you   and   I
        gusto mo nang meet
            sa swing set
                    katabi yung old bahay mo?

                    maupo tayo sa black rubber seats
                    and listen to the sound of metal clinking
                    as we spin round

                    only for the other to
                    release the coil.

My time as a goldfish

I rode around   in a fishbowl   the road beneath:
solid,   smooth,   black.   When my bike's wheels met
     and startled rocks   they crackled.

The wind kept me company and   rushed
     in time   with my rotating legs
                    as I followed   the bowl's boundary.
     It brushed   my hair,   tugged and swirled
          each strand into the ebony night.

If the moon had been any bigger   it would have   reached
     down and pressed   a spearmint kiss to my forehead.
The tops of my knees   grazed   the handle bars,
rubbery,   and ridged   inside my palm.

Memories of rain

I had seen torrential rain bring
planks for damming and rats
to run from.

I had watched papa N trudge
through water for a ciggie to keep
toxins out of the house.

I had heard mama F warn
not to follow or else the rats
would bite.

I was fast asleep
when a cockroach bit
my upper lip

causing a swell of red to
make funny incomplete words
for a short stretch of days.

I was in my summer uniform
when I looked up, asked the Teacher,

Is this snow?

No, it doesn't snow in
this part of Australia.
This is rain. It's sprinkling.

I had never seen snow
nor ever known rain, soft and melting;
powdering indiscriminately.

I held out my hand to catch
it for papa N and mama F
maybe I could

place each dainty droplet in a globe,
pack it for a plane
headed home to Malabon.

You don't look filo

If I'm honest,
I downplayed my beauty
as *generic*
asian features
to try and dissipate
some confused expressions
at a spin-the-goon-on-the-Hills-Hoist-party

If I'm honest,
I'm too frothy for the inevitable game of,
'Guess where I'm from'
coz no one ever can.
And when I say, *I'm Filo*,
people like to follow up, correct me,
But, like, halfie, *right?*

If I’m honest,
I’m a greedy child sampling
each sweet shock
on everyone’s face
when I say,
Nope. I’m full Filo.

And if I'm honest,
I have goldfish lips and matching
protruding eyes. I see
men wave with zealous shouts of *Ni Hao*
and I always reply
with my equally enthusiastic middle finger.

ambrosial waves

after Jazz Money

*

like
a part
of my circadian
rhythm i recurrently
sit at the highest peak
of a sloping cliff
composed of a
meadow

*

the grass
on the meadow
rustles. tranquillity
lulls from the
gloom. this
realm is
mine.

*

i stare up
into a dark
tulle interlaced
with a nebula blanket
cradling scintillating light.
it is often overshadowed by
the pale bloom of the moon.
a cool breeze imbues the
air in this world
of eternal
night.

*

ponderous
sighs slip in small
blithe moments held
between lithe movements
of memories mirroring sallow
replayings of a previous life.
the turbulent memories
are subdued
on
isles
surrounded by
ambrosial waves. the
memories are chained to the
earth, enclosed under thick,
opaque glossed domes
that reflect nothing
but the
sky

*

when the
moon breathes a little
too close it is easier to
ignore the valley at the
bottom of the cliff that
bears a looming
mansion.

*

the
only part i
have glimpsed:
the second floor, an
endless sombre passage
sheathed on both sides with
wooden doors i have never
intentionally opened but
always unmistakably
close.

*

i never
stay more than
a mood and even then
my body remains
upon the
cliff.

*

the
feelings
of agony, anxiety
which sporadically
escape from the
domes
are
gently
suffocated
by the ocean
whose sonorous
hushings leave
the atmosphere
nostalgic

*

I nearly crushed my dog to death

- ode to gigil (*n. "geeh-gihl"*)

In use:
I was so full of gigil that I nearly
crushed my dog to death.

It's a simple enough emotion
pre-empting the intake of air
in preparation for the battle
with one's own body
to find the happy medium
between fractured bones
and sufficiently squeezed.

It's the advancing drumbeat
marching outward
employing each limb to move and wrap
around the subject. Frequently
involving intimate proximity
cheek stamped cheek
lips, missiles, locked on
to make a wriggly worm out of them.

In use:
gigil took over my body, suddenly
I was squishing my toddler, rubbing his
cheeks with mine and giving him smoochies!
He was being too cute!

It's the flurry of uncontainable love
immeasurable affection. To hold the centre
of it is to ensure they exist.
In their existence
both hearts, unintentionally, gratifyingly,
saturates past full
so both can watch the puddles expand
rejoice in ripples, step in splash
be amazed by the wonder
and reflect: *such a beautiful being*
is here with me.

Frankie, the cat.

Born in May,
my purring ball of sweetness has marked
the passing days with tufts of fur,
forcing time to stick to me, routinely,
(the way my psychiatrist prescribed
but not quite)
through feedings and play and
cuddles between her flopping in rays.

The sun blinks through shades
of storms, kneading this year's seasons
into the colour of her relaxed future
cake made of tuna, salmon, and
mackerel treats - a surprise
homing beacon for her whiskers and nose
as pink as the secrets
of her paws.

I'll fashion her a crown of falling
auburn leaves, take a string
from an old pair of shorts and squiggle it across the carpet;
knotted kisses for her to rush after.

I'll watch her try to evade my arms with
her half-hearted rebellion inciting my now
never ceasing laughter.

I'll thank her for sandwiching my leg
with her tiny toes which grants me an anchor
during mood swings, rememberings, therapy.

I find my own birthday
a little daunting
but hers is two days before
with endless possibility; wishes;
opportunity; permission; chance and
the nuzzle of being chosen.

She is heart-shaped
as she lends my feet some warmth
then yawning, walking toward my head
to bop, bop it with hers. Before
posing in stretch and extending
her snooze on my chest.

Flame Bowerbird

I am

furore, glossed flame,
entranced by the rainforest

almost indecent, you see   beyond skin
deeper than marrow
deeper in ghost

laway strings

let me nestle in your lung's capillaries
tuck me in   to your grey matter,
I'll make myself at home

drink deep
from the pulse of my pupils

You, reader.
You are exactly
where I want you.

watch my humantics
my rhythmic blaze
how I dare danger

then I'll

untog

untog untog

the bird that could not fly

- for me

she may have germinated by accident
        as many of us do
        as a bird made of bark and no
wings she cannot swivel
        she cannot dive
        she cannot   not   not

what is the use in trying

that thought returns periodically
as persistent as earth's breath
blasting away her leaves

B
E
N
D
I
N
G

her N

then W   SE

E   sometimes SWS

then N again

before settling
to sway her to sleep

after each luteal phase she discovers
ways to reach the sky
by allowing each stiff stubborn
part to fuse and splint
-er as they like

forming infinite phalanges
she practises
what she learnt from hoarding
breezes gusts and hurricanes how to
tenderly seize soggy
clouds foreboding asphyxiating how to
cautiously catch droplets
that seed
and swell amidst her ribs
her outstretched rustling arms
whistle serendipitously off

key i cannot

promise it will be a pleasant
encounter but I invite you

to sit and watch her
as she makes her crown and adorns it with

visions of
psp   psp-ing
all the cats   walking by

her evergreen root hairs stubbing
against metamorphic rocks

falling in love with
her annual rings

everyth i ng
n

b

e
tw en

IV.

DÉJÀ RÊVÉ

We bought a star

SUNDAY 20TH DEC 4037: 12:12

We
bought
it from the
same store every
family goes to.

The star with its
withered limbs,
was almost dying. We took it home,
and slipped off the packaging that read:

Real Authentic Stars, mined
straight from the sky!

Mum put on the instructional video. At 13,
it was time I learnt to make the ornamental tree topper.
I hollowed it out, scraped its night-bleeding insides with a
butter knife. I watched dark sapphire quark soup ooze into the
disposal bag marked:
Biohazard.
The bag was only an extra dollar fifty.

"*It was already emaciated, starved of joy, so there's no need to worry.*
You haven't done a bad thing," the man in the video said.

Copying the instructor, I blew open the husk, huffed in my carbon dioxide; set it in
resin and coated it in glitter.

It will shimmer in silver for us before the end of the year.

"*You gave it new life*."

And what of the glitter
that falls down the drain?
My family and I sang in
tune with the screen,

'The fish will thank us for the sparkle in their scales!'

J. Marahuyo

J. Marahuyo is a neurodivergent Filipino-Australian award winning poet.
She was shortlisted for the Newcastle Poetry Prize 2024,
won the Writing NSW-Varuna Fellowship 2024 and won the Living Stories Prize 2024.
crying gorgeously; 4:37am is her debut collection.

Notes

Living within the accretion disk: Based on black holes and the accretion disk surrounding them.

Fistfuls of Sand: Tala refers to popular Tagalog myth, she is the Goddess of stars.
Living within the Event Horizon: Based on black holes and the event horizons surrounding them.

ambrosial waves: the structure of the poem is inspired by Jazz Money's poem 'if the ghost is still here come morning' which can be found on Cordite Poetry review.

meeting Amihan: This is an ekphrastic poem based on a painting called Garden of Love, by Remedios Varo, 1951. Referenced is the myth of Amihan, a Tagalog tale, who is considered to be the first being in the universe.

Flame Bowerbird: based on the documentary 'Dancing with the Birds', the phrase 'where I want you' has been inspired by & rephrased from the narration.

Infinite Blue Candies and *Eyeballs*: makes references to the story of *Snow White*, and *The Golden Goose.* Buwan is a character from Tagalog mythology, from the story, 'Why the sun is brighter than the moon.' Panaoptes is a many-eyed giant in Greek mythology.

ba-ad ba-ad black sheep: based on the nursery rhyme with *Snow White* references.

Acknowledgements

I write and live on Dharug land and would like to pay my respects to the First Nations peoples the Dharug, Gundungurra, Wanaruah, Wiradjuri, Darkinjung, and Tharawal people, their elders past and present of so-called Sydney, Australia.

I cannot express how grateful I am to the following organisations and people who have supported my journey as a poet and the birth of this collection. Thank you to my mentor ali whitelock who oversaw this entire collection, giving me endless hours and all the warmth and encouragement a baby poet could ever hope for.

Thank you to WestWords, especially Ally Burnham and Michael Campbell, for introducing me to and helping me forge connections within the Western Sydney writing community through the various programs and events it regularly hosts, the first I encountered being WestWords Academy. This program provided me with the tools necessary to take being a writer and poet seriously, I gained invaluable knowledge about the nitty-gritty admin side and how it is essentially running your own business, without the monthly sessions keeping me accountable and connected I would not have the network I currently have. Their industry knowledge connected me with someone who was able to understand this collection and my work in general so that I could thrive, my dearest mentor ali whitelock. WestWords' belief in me has nourished my growth and their team has created so many opportunities for me to share my work with the wider community by hosting numerous competitions, workshops and performance opportunities. I have been lucky enough to enter or take part in countless opportunities as more often than not the team has ensured one of the major barriers to participation, that is, financial, is greatly reduced or non-existent, this includes: Living Stories annual writing competition, the WestWords-Cumberland Women's Health writing workshop program, WestWords-Varuna Emerging Writers Residency, WestWords Academy Night Live!, WestWords x First Draft, Slam Messiah by WestWords and River City Voices, Blacktown Mayoral writing prize. Their partnership with West Side Poetry Slam and their workshops hosted by several well-respected poets over the years has provided me with a space to connect and share my work. Other opportunities include performing at Granville Nights 2023, After Dark at the Police and Justice Museum 2023, Being Differently at WestWords 2023; speaking as a panellist for Emerging Voices: the new writers of Western Sydney at the Art Gallery of NSW 2022, and for Diversity Festival at Western Sydney University 2024. I have also had the pleasure of judging and hosting workshops in schools thanks to this phenomenal organisation including Blacktown Mayoral prize 2024. I am truly grateful to this small but powerful and passionate team for their belief in my work which has ultimately led me to publish with them under their imprint WestWords Books. Again, super special thanks to Michael Campbell for your time and efforts in editing, understanding my antics and taking care of all the logistics of the book production. Thank you WestWords and WestWords Books, you have my eternal gratitude for helping me achieve my dreams <3.

Thank you to Varuna National Writers House for the creative space, and exquisite dinners which I was lucky to experience thanks to the fellowship WestWords-Varuna Emerging Writers Residency, 2022. Thank you for Express Media for choosing me for the 2022 Toolkits Lite: Poetry mentorship program, providing me with connections, encouragement and feedback. Thank you to The Writing and Research Centre of Western Sydney for selecting me for The Writing Zone mentorship program, especially Kate Fagan, Melinda Jewell and Ellen O'Brien, for their warmth, care and editorial advice throughout 2022-23.

Thank you to Harvey Liu and my sister Lashu for being my first readers alongside my mentor ali whitelock. Your insights, mutual ramblings and support is what has brought this collection to life. Thank you to ate p for cross-checking the tagalog in this collection, you have helped me grow immensely. Thank you to my sister Wynter for her distractions and emotional support. Thank you to all the women in my life who have cared, cried with me and held me and who have shared their vulnerabilities in turn. And finally thank you to the following publications which several poems of the collection have appeared in in previous versions:

- Dancing Dragons Romanian/Australian anthology,
- FemAsia magazine, *Twice as Many Stars* anthology,
- *Living Stories: The Other City* anthology,
- *The Space Between* chapbook, Alice Sinclair's
- *Out of the Shadows* anthology,

- Poetica Christi Press *Transformation* anthology,
- Alice Sinclair's *Out of the Shadows* anthology,
- Short Stories Unlimited *Four Seasons* anthology
- *The Space Between* chapbook,
- Alice Sinclair's *Out of the Shadows* anthology
- *Poetry of Encounter: The Liquid Amber Prize* anthology,
- *ZineWest* 2022 and 2024,
- Born Writers Award website,
- *Living Stories: Things Unsaid* anthology,
- *Cordite Poetry Review*,
- *Cat Anthology* by Illographo Press,
- *Blacktown Mayoral Creative Writing Prize: EXTRAordinary,*
- *Locative* zine,
- *Gems* zine,
- Kyogle Festival website,
- *Undoing* anthology,
- *Out of the Shadows* anthology,
- *Moss Puppy* magazine,
- *Written Off*

Salamat po to all you readers and lovers of poetry, I hope you feel all your feels and find clarity in the space between. J.